The Church's
Folk Songs

From *Hymns Ancient & Modern*
to *Common Praise*
1861–2011

Trevor Beeson

CANTERBURY
PRESS
Norwich

© Trevor Beeson 2011

Published in 2011 by Canterbury Press

Editorial office
13–17 Long Lane,
London, EC1A 9PN, UK

Canterbury Press is an imprint of Hymns Ancient and Modern Ltd
(a registered charity)
13a Hellesdon Park Road, Norwich, Norfolk, NR6 5DR

www.scm-canterburypress.co.uk

British Library Cataloguing in Publication data

A catalogue record for this book is available
from the British Library

978 1 84825 107 6

Typeset by Regent Typesetting

Printed and bound by
Halstan & Co Ltd, Amersham, Bucks

Contents

CHAPTER ONE

Starting on the Great Western

A carriage on the old Great Western Railway might seem an improbable place for advancing a revolution in the Church of England's worship. But so it proved to be, and it concerned the singing of hymns, an element which had been neglected for more than two centuries.

It was in the summer of 1858 that two enthusiastic collectors of hymns, old and new, found themselves in the same railway carriage and took the opportunity to discuss their work. The Revd William Denton, Vicar of St Bartholomew, Cripplegate, in the City of London, was the editor of a successful *Church Hymnal* which had been published five years earlier. The Revd Francis Murray, Vicar of St Nicholas, Chislehurst, in Kent, had compiled with the assistance of his curate, the Revd Charles Harrison, *A Hymnal for use in the English Church*. Published six years earlier, this contained 158 hymns and had sold 20,000 copies in three editions.

Arising from their conversation the two priests, both influenced by the Oxford Movement, decided to convene a meeting of other hymn writers, composers and editors to see if it might be possible to bring together their work to form a single hymn book that would be of service to the whole church. Little time was lost and an exploratory meeting was arranged in the clergy house at St Barnabas, Pimlico, in London, where the curate-in-charge, the Revd George Cosby White, a former curate of Chislehurst, had also compiled a book of *Hymns and Introits* (1852) for the high church All Saints, Margaret Street, in London's West End. Besides Murray, C. R. Harrison, another former Chislehurst curate, and Cosby White, Sir Henry Baker, the baronet Vicar of Monkland, Herefordshire, and his neighbour, the Revd W. Pulling, Vicar of Eastnor, were present, but owing to a misunderstanding Denton was not invited. He never became involved in the project, though this may have been more to do with unwillingness to surrender control of his own book.

Nonetheless it was decided to go ahead and Baker was appointed secretary of the continuing committee, to which were added the Revd William Richards, Vicar of All Saints, Margaret Street, the Revd George Huntingford, Vicar of Littlemore, Oxford (famed for its earlier associations with John Henry Newman) and the Revd John Woodford, a future Bishop of Ely. An advertisement inviting collaboration was placed in the *Guardian* (an influential church paper of the time) and brought a considerable response, mainly from clergy who were busy compiling their own books. Inevitably, they had many different ideas about the character and contents of the proposed publication.

John Keble, the founder of the Oxford Movement and author of the best-selling *The Christian Year*, counselled 'If you desire to make a hymn book for the use of the whole church, make it comprehensive.' He declined an invitation to join the committee but agreed to be an adviser and some of his poems, 'New every morning is the love', 'Blest are the pure in heart', 'Son of my soul, thou Saviour dear' and 'When God of old came down from heaven' became well loved hymns. The Revd John Mason Neale, a highly gifted priest and translator, offered his services and made a vital contribution. From the outset it was determined that the book would be designed not only as an aid to worship but also as a means of teaching the Catholic faith. Hymns were intended to be said as well as sung, so that a hymn book became for Victorians a manual of doctrine and devotion, something to be used in the home as well as in church.

In the end the size of the committee was increased to about 20 and in May 1859 a test booklet of 50 hymns was circulated for comment, followed by an enlarged version. In October of the following year Baker announced that a words edition of a book containing 273 hymns would be published on Advent Sunday and an edition with tunes on 20 March 1861 – less than three years after the railway carriage conversation.

This was a very short time in which to make the skilful, sensitive choice of material for so important a breakthrough in the content of the church's worship. But considerable care was taken over the choices, the order of the Christian year was followed, each hymn was headed by an appropriate Biblical text (though not the names of the authors and composers) and it is significant that only a few of the original 273 were discarded as late as the 1950 edition. Without enthusiasm, energy and drive, particularly on the part of Baker, the project may in any case never have got off the ground, and the committee was rewarded with massive sales. The music edition sold one hundred thousand copies in the first year and by 1868 sales totalled four and a half million. It was obviously meeting a need. The cheapest words edition, bound in cloth boards, cost 4d and the cheapest music edition 1s 2d.

Hymns Ancient & Modern, as it was called, was on its way to becoming a national institution. By the end of the century, sales would exceed 35 million copies. And it was not only a national institution, for missionaries carried copies of it to the ends of the earth where, often incongruously, the hymns were sung in the depths of Central Africa and the mysterious lands of the Orient. They became an expression, not only of the Christian Gospel, but also of British imperialism. The title, usually credited to Dr W. H. Monk, the music editor, accurately described the committee's aims which, in common with those of the Oxford Movement, were concerned to get behind the Reformation to the Church's earlier years. Thus, of the 273 hymns in the first edition, 110 were translations from Latin.

The choice of Monk as music editor was inspired. He was organist and director of music at King's College London and immediately aware that the finest words were of little use unless congregations were drawn into song by means of appropriate, singable tunes. He had a remarkable gift for making right choices and staked a claim to worldwide fame by composing the tune *Eventide* for H. F. Lyte's 'Abide with me'. He also contributed many more, including those commonly used for Mrs C. F. Alexander's 'All things bright and beautiful' and Charles Wesley's 'Hail the day that sees him rise' and 'Soldiers of Christ, arise' – in all there are 17 in *Common Praise*.

Although *Hymns Ancient & Modern* was an immediate publishing success and had a transforming effect on the Church of England's worship, not everyone was happy with it. Some bishops and theologians, suspicious of its Oxford Movement spirit, had little difficulty in detecting here and there what they regarded as heresy. Frances Ridley Havergal, herself a prolific hymnwriter of intense evangelical piety, and best remembered for her 'Take my life, and let it be', warned that the book was 'The thin edge of the wedge of Popery'. When rebuked by a friend and mentor for even looking at it, she explained that she had only glanced at some of the music in the 1868 Supplement. Others regretted that there was not more of Isaac Watts and Charles Wesley, while some musicians were appalled by 'low grade sentimental tunes'.

Criticism of this sort attended the next few editions and indeed every other hymn book of whatever tradition. This was, and remains, inevitable since personal needs and tastes vary considerably and hymns are too important to be exempt from opinion. This raises the wider issue of what level of poetry and music is necessary for the church's folk music. All hymn book editors have wrestled with this question and been driven to include hymns that they would have preferred to leave out, but could not because the particular hymns had become so popular and evidently met a need.

Another issue that arose early and has faced editors ever since concerns their liberty to alter hymns. At a Nottingham church congress in 1871 Bishop Christopher Wordsworth of Lincoln publicly attacked the compilers of the 1868 supplement for shortening his 'O Lord of heaven and earth and sea', but omission of particular verses of hymns became, and remains, commonplace. The 1888 editors may perhaps be excused for leaving out of 'Thy hand, O God, has guided' the verse:

God bless our merry England,
   God bless our Church and Queen,
God bless our great Archbishop,
   The best there's ever been.

More serious is the changing of words, usually to replace archaisms, but sometimes, in modern evangelical collections, also to change doctrine, which must always be unacceptable. Changes to embrace inclusive gender language are now common and some brave, but misguided, editors have even dared to tamper with the poetry of George Herbert.

The 1868 supplement contained 113 hymns, mainly the work of contemporary writers and composers, and displayed considerable skill in matching words and appropriate tunes. Many of these are now regarded as inseparable. In the following year work began on a revised edition which appeared in 1875 with 473 hymns. But the demand for more was insatiable, so another supplement was added in 1889; this sold one million copies on the day of its publication and another two and a half million by the end of the following year.

Other hymns books remained in circulation, but by now 70 per cent of the parishes were using *Hymns Ancient & Modern* and there was talk and some negotiations over the possibility of it becoming the Church of England's official hymn book. It seemed anomalous to many that the Church's liturgy should be controlled by Act of Parliament while no less influential hymnody was open to a free for all. Fortunately, for the sake of creativity, the negotiations came to nothing, though later the *Book of Common Prayer* and *Hymns Ancient & Modern* were often bound together for personal use. They still are.

The issue of quality would not however go away and, although the proofs of the latest edition had been read by the Archbishop of Canterbury, Edward White Benson, it was given a particularly hostile reception by the *Church Quarterly Review* which complained, 'The book is marked by poverty of thought and diction, the work of versifiers rather than poets.'

The publication in 1906 of the *English Hymnal* was a deliberate attempt to raise standards, and in his preface the music editor, none other than the then young Ralph Vaughan Williams, declared music for worship to be 'a moral issue' and added, pointedly, 'It ought no longer to be anywhere that the most exalted moments of a churchgoer's week are associated with music that would not be tolerated in any place of secular entertainment.' He was ruthless in his own choices but had to include some hymns and tunes in an appendix which he described as his 'chamber of horrors'.

Among the recent appointments as proprietors (as they had come to be called) of *Hymns Ancient & Modern* there were however two distinguished scholars, Walter Howard Frere, of the Community of the Resurrection and Bishop of Truro, and Arthur James Mason, of Canterbury and Cambridge, who were no less conscious of the weakness of much Victorian hymnody and played a leading part in one more revision which had been started in 1895. The music committee of this had Frere as chairman and included Charles Villiers Stanford, Charles Wood and other leading composers of the time, so when the new edition appeared in 1904 it was evident that more exacting standards had been applied.

The Times commented, 'The tunes which appeal most to domestic servants are all, or nearly all, retained, but the book is a very great advance on the old.' The *Church Times* was glad to see the back of 'the sugary and lackadaisical tunes and the feeble ditties to which they were wedded'. But although it eventually sold two million copies it was, in a sense, too good to be truly popular. It did not go down well in village churches where changes and omissions were attributed to pedantry rather than to a quest for excellence, and replacement involved more expense. A supplement of discarded tunes was rushed into print and it was explained that the former edition would remain available for those who preferred it.

The proprietors had shortly before this found themselves accused, in a *Church Times* editorial, headed 'A Conspiracy Unearthed', of planning 'a new and watered down edition' to supplant the existing editions and, by thus conciliating Protestant opinion, produce a single hymn book acceptable to the whole church. This they indignantly denied.

Another supplement was published in 1916 and what was described as the Standard Edition, containing 778 hymns, followed in 1922. A further revision, started in 1938, and intended to include some of the twentieth century's hymns, was impeded by the outbreak of the 1939–45 war.

CHAPTER TWO

All Change in a Changing Church

When the proprietors resumed their work in earnest in 1945 they were soon to lose Sir Sydney Nicholson, a former Organist and Master of the Choristers at Westminster Abbey and the renowned founder of the Royal School of Church Music. He was appointed in 1928 – the first layman to be chosen – and ten years later became chairman. But after spending the war years travelling the country on an motorcycle to keep parish church choirs alive, he died in 1947.

This was a serious blow since he had an unrivalled knowledge of English church music and a special empathy with the parishes. He was succeeded as a proprietor by John Dykes Bower, the organist of St Paul's Cathedral, while Canon William Lowther Clarke, a liturgist of Chichester Cathedral, took over as chairman.

The purpose of the revision was refinement of the 1904 edition, cutting out the dead wood, of which there was now a great deal, adding a modest number of new hymns, and reducing the size to about 600 – in the event, 634. When it appeared in 1950 the Preface explained: 'The new book does not aim at breaking fresh ground or exploiting novel ideas.'

Still recovering from a catastrophic war, the church was believed to be unready for much change, so the book created none of the criticism and controversy that greeted some of its predecessors. Sales were not sensational, but they were good enough; in a small volume published to commemorate the centenary of *Hymns Ancient & Modern* in 1961, Canon Lowther Clarke estimated that total sales of all editions were of the order of 150 million.

The scale and speed of this advance, particularly during the nineteenth century, together with the impressive progress of the hymn books of other churches, offers clear evidence of the impact made by hymnody on English life and culture. Its transforming effect on the life of the church cannot be exaggerated. There was more to be achieved in the twentieth century through new biblical insights into the nature of the church and the centrality of the Eucharist, but corporate hymn singing provided a preliminary breakthrough in the church's understanding of itself.

The Hymn Society of Great Britain and Ireland, founded by a group of enthusiasts in 1936, now flourishes as never before. Its aims are to encourage study and research into hymns, both words and music, and, no less important, good standards of hymn singing and the discerning choice of hymns in worship. It publishes a quarterly magazine and has an annual conference.

The extent to which secularization has now penetrated modern British culture is often debated. In the 2001 population census 72 per cent claimed allegiance to Christianity but between 1947 and 2000 the number of those attending Church of England services halved. In 1960 about 70 per cent of the population was baptized in infancy; by the end of the century this had been reduced to about 25 per cent. In 1951 there were 18,196 Anglican clergy; in 2000 there were 10,700, including 2,000 women priests.

Nonetheless, the church's contribution to society is still considerable, through its 16,000 places of worship, 4,700 schools and deep involvement in many aspects of social and community life. And over the last 50 years it has embraced considerable change, most noticeably in the realm of worship where, in the overwhelming majority of parishes of all traditions, the Eucharist has replaced choral mattins as the chief, and sometimes the only, act of Sunday worship. This has been accompanied by the most extensive liturgical changes since the Reformation, and often led to the re-ordering of church buildings to facilitate more active participation by the whole congregation.

The consequences of this for hymnody have been considerable and its importance increased by the new emphasis on congregational involvement. The decline of parish church choirs, a serious loss in some ways, has in many places required congregations to work harder and sing louder. Hymn book compilers have been required to provide a much larger choice of hymns appropriate to the Eucharist. Although a product of the Oxford Movement, the first edition of *Hymns Ancient & Modern* provided only five of these, since choral Eucharists were then virtually unknown. The 1950 revision offered 42 and *Common*

Praise has 67, together with suggestions of appropriate hymns for every Sunday of the year to match the three-year biblical lectionary of *Common Worship*, the Church's most recent service book.

Looking beyond the Church's own worship, it is no longer the case that hymn singing is as pervasive an element in English social life as it became in the Victorian era, when families gathered around a piano or a harmonium at home to sing and when hymns were sung in halls, pubs and other meeting places. Even secular organizations felt the need to compile their own godless books. Yet hymn singing remains a widely spread activity and still features in a great variety of community and personal events.

'Abide with me' was first sung, with the strong approval of King George V, at the FA Cup Final in 1927 and still provides what is seen as a fitting conclusion to the community singing before the game starts. Equally, *Jerusalem*, often treated as an alternative national anthem, is an indispensable item at the Last Night of the Proms as well as the unofficial anthem of the secular Women's Institute. Hymns are sung at war memorials and by soldiers still facing danger in current wars. They continue to be sung in schools and at the weddings and funerals of non-churchgoers.

Songs of Praise, the BBC's flagship religious television programme devoted to hymn singing, was first broadcast in 1962 and now has about three million viewers, one million fewer than a decade ago. More than any other programme of any sort, it attracts active audience participation. In many nursing and care homes it provides the regular Sunday worship. Just over half of viewers are aged 65 and over, but 1.3 million are under 45. Gordon Brown, the then Prime Minister, made an appearance in 2009, having been advised that this was a valuable opportunity to strengthen contact with 'middle England'. Among the national millennium celebrations in 2000 a *Songs of Praise,* broadcast from a stadium in Cardiff, attracted 66,000 participants, including the Prince of Wales and his sons, Prince William and Prince Harry. Cliff Richard sang his *Millennium Prayer*. The programme went to South Africa in 2010 as a prelude to the opening there of football's World Cup.

Back in the 1970s, Yorkshire Television's *Stars on Sundays* competed with *Songs of Praise* for the mass Sunday evening audience. Described by one critic as 'Sunday Night at the London Palladium with a hymn book', it had a very large following, but came to an end in 1979. This was just as well, since another critic concluded, 'This show did more to promote atheism in Britain than any other, before or since'. It was succeeded by *Highway* – a fairly straightforward offering of favourite hymns and religious songs presented by Harry Secombe, usually from churches and cathedrals. This became a casualty of the reduction in religious broadcasting.

Longer lived than any of these and of most other broadcasts is BBC Radio 2's *Sunday Half Hour*. First heard during the dark, wartime days of 1940, it now includes discussion and prayers as well as request hymns, and is apparently indestructible on the BBC's most popular radio channel.

So, in a world very different from that of 1861, the Church's folk songs are still alive and well, and their development over the changing scenes of Christian history has been remarkable.

CHAPTER THREE

Hymnody's Origins and Development

Christians have from the earliest days worshipped God and expressed their faith in song. St Mark's Gospel records that after the Last Supper, Jesus and the eleven apostles 'sang a hymn and went out to the Mount of Olives'. This was probably the Jewish *Hallel* consisting of Psalms 113–118, used at the Passover, and there are other New Testament references to the use of the Psalms, these being the hymns of the Jewish faith. But the New Testament also differentiates hymns from psalms and some scholars believe that fragments of early Christian hymns are to be found in St Paul's letters.

In AD 110 Pliny, a Roman governor, reported to the Emperor that Christians in Bythinia were 'singing to Christ as God', and a third-century writer referred to 'psalms and odes such were from the beginning written by believers, hymns to the Christ, the Word of God, calling him God'. The earliest hymn still in use dates back to the Greek branch of the third-century church and may be even earlier. John Keble was the translator:

Hail, gladdening Light, of his pure glory poured
who is the immortal Father, heavenly, blest,
holiest of holies, Jesus Christ our Lord.

Now we are come to the sun's hour of rest,
the lights of evening round us shine,
we hymn the Father, Son, and Holy Spirit divine.

Worthiest art thou at all times to be sung
with undefiled tongue:
Son of God, giver of life, alone:
therefore in all the world thy glories, Lord, they own.

During the fourth century, hymns were widely used to express and propagate the beliefs of the rival parties in a great controversy about the divine/human nature of Christ. Heresy, it was alleged, was spread by singing boatmen on the Nile. In the same century Ambrose, Bishop of Milan, composed and got others to compose, in Latin, what became known as 'office hymns'. These were for use at certain designated places in the church's services – a practice still widely observed, especially in monastic communities.

Of Ambrose's own hymns, 'O splendour of God's glory bright', 'O strength and stay upholding all creation', and, for Christmas, 'Come, thou Redeemer of the earth' are still much used. His influence on the development of hymn singing was considerable, as it was on Augustine of Hippo who wrote in his *Confessions* (398–400):

> It was at this time that the practice was instituted [at Milan] of singing hymns and psalms after the manner of the Eastern churches, to keep the people from being altogether worn out with anxiety and want of sleep. The custom has been retained from that day to this, and has been imitated by many, indeed in almost all, congregations throughout the world.

By the seventh century, hymns were being written in Britain. Caedmon, a monk of Whitby and the earliest known English Christian poet, produced a hymn that was, he said, composed in a dream. During the next two centuries Bishop Aldhelm and King Alfred the Great also wrote hymns and throughout the Middle Ages there was a good deal of Latin hymn writing all over Western Europe.

Stephen Langton, Archbishop of Canterbury (1207–28), bequeathed to us 'Come, thou Holy Spirit, come' while in the previous century in France Peter Abelard, a great scholar monk, gave as a parting gift to his beloved Héloïse a book of 93 of his own hymns for use by the nuns in her convent. Three of these are in *Common Praise*, easily the best known being O *Quanta Qualia* in J. M. Neale's inspired translation, which begins:

> O what their joy and their glory must be,
> those endless sabbaths the blessed ones see;
> crown for the valiant, to weary ones rest;
> God shall be all, and in all ever blest.

The tune is an adaptation of a medieval French plainchant which sings even better when used with the original Latin. Among the many others from that era, 'Jerusalem the golden' by Bernard of Cluny, 'Come down, O Love divine' by Bianco of Siena, and 'Ye choirs of new Jerusalem' by St Fulbert of Chartres are specially notable and all exhibit the combination of spiritual insight and poetic gift which is the mark of the best hymnody.

Hymns and other church music were then, however, largely confined to monasteries and collegiate churches where there was a disciplined approach to singing, though laypeople were often encouraged to join in the singing of a hymn to the Virgin at a short late-afternoon service. On the whole, though, there was little of the Latin services for them to sing in their parish churches, until the late Middle Ages. Then the singing of carols in English – for all seasons of the year, not just for Christmas – was authorized, and a rich outpouring of these ensued. Today's Christmas Services of Nine Lessons with Carols indicate the quality and enduring quality of many of them.

Yet it was not until the Reformation of the sixteenth and seventeenth centuries that there came a breakthrough in congregational verbal participation in worship. Hymn singing was a critical element in this and Erik Routley said, 'It was the medievals who showed us what hymns could do; it was the Reformers who showed us how to use them'.

Martin Luther (1483–1546), the greatest theologian of the Reformation, was also a poet and a musician. He, too, recognized that hymns could express a corporate Christian identity and also help to spread a message. So he wrote some himself, composed tunes for the work of others, and initiated a remarkable era of German hymnody. When translators eventually got to work, this enriched the worship and personal devotion of the entire Christian world.

A collection of German hymns published in 1524 consisted mainly of material based on the Psalms and was replete with strong Reformation doctrine. Luther's own, 'A safe stronghold our God is still', for which he composed the tune *Ein' feste Burg* (later harmonized by J. S. Bach), was first published in 1529. Its use spread quickly throughout Germany and it has been described as 'the Marseillaise of the Reformation', becoming also an expression of German nationalism. Henry VIII forbade its use in England because of his aversion to Lutherism. It begins, and continues, majestically:

A safe stronghold our God is still,
   a trusty shield and weapon;
he'll keep us clear from all the ill
   that hath us now o'ertaken.

and ends triumphantly:

The City of God remaineth.

Other magnificent German offerings include 'Wake, O wake! With tidings thrilling', written by a pastor, Philipp Nicolai, during a desperate time of plague in his parish, 'Now thank we all our God', 'Praise to the Lord, the Almighty, the King of creation', and 'Ah, holy Jesu, how hast thou offended' – all greatly enhanced by their tunes. At one time virtually every local community in Germany had its own compiled hymnal, made possible by the invention of printing.

But John Calvin (1509–64) of Geneva, the other great theologian of the Reformation, would have none of this – not because his sombre beliefs made him averse to music and singing, but simply because he believed that only biblical material was acceptable in worship. His hymnody was therefore confined to the Psalms and these were turned into metrical form so that they could be used with singable, hymn-like tunes. A Genevan school of church music was thus inaugurated.

In England, Thomas Cranmer, the architect of the *Book of Common Prayer*, was concerned essentially to produce a revised, vernacular and unadorned version of the long-established liturgy. At the same time, he was aware that he lacked the skill the translate the old Latin hymns into graceful, poetic English. So he prescribed only that at morning and evening prayer an anthem might by used 'in choirs and places where they sing'.

An important consequence of Queen Mary Tudor's persecution of Protestants was to drive a significant number of them to the Continent, and especially to the more hospitable Geneva. There they learned to sing and appreciate the metrical psalms and on their return to England after the accession of Queen Elizabeth I in 1558 they brought these with them.

Thomas Sternhold, MP for Plymouth, and John Hopkins, a Suffolk clergyman, began to produce English translations and a complete edition of the Psalter was published in 1562. Congregations now had something to sing in church, but it was not the sort of Christian folk music to express or encourage the belief that in Christ lay the secret of abundant life. Much of it was exceedingly dreary. A later version, however, produced by two Irishmen, Nahum Tate and Nicholas Brady in 1696, included a few versifications of psalms, such as 'All people that on earth do dwell', 'Through all the changing scenes of life' and 'As pants the heart for cooling streams'. These became popular and were good enough to survive into the twenty-first century.

While the standard of cathedral choirs varied considerably in the second half of the eighteenth century, numerous settings and anthems were written by distinguished composers, including William Boyce and Maurice Greene. Most town churches had organs by the end of the century, often with choirs who sang settings of canticles at Sunday morning and evening prayer, and sometimes of the Sanctus and Gloria at monthly celebrations of Holy Communion. Metrical psalms and scriptural paraphrases were sung between morning prayer, the Litany and Holy Communion. Many town parishes published their own collections of hymns and psalm tunes.

There was sometimes tension between clergy, wanting choirs to lead congregational singing, and choirs wishing to demonstrate their musical abilities. In villages, parish clerks led metrical psalms, but they also had groups of singers, and sometimes, from the early nineteenth century, small orchestras. Children from parish charity schools were also often taught to sing metrical psalms in church. Bishops encouraged singing to compete with Methodism. In the early nineteenth century much simple music was published for church choirs.

CHAPTER FOUR

Breaking the Long Silence

The Church's folk songs could not be silenced, however and when
they reappeared in the eighteenth century in a different, vernacular
form they came from the voice of Dissent, within and without the
Established Church. Their tone was that of a rising evangelical movement which recognized the vital importance of full congregational
participation in worship and at the same time the need for Christians
to express corporately their personal experiences of faith, sometimes
emotionally.

Isaac Watts (1674–1748)

Isaac Watts is universally recognized as 'the father of English hymnody'. He wrote 750 hymns, many of which went into the first edition
of *Hymns Ancient & Modern*, and 28 remain in *Common Praise*. Free
Church hymnals include much larger numbers and there can be few
churches in the English-speaking world that do not make frequent use
of 'When I survey the wondrous cross' (believed by many to be the
greatest of all hymns), 'O God, our help in ages past' and 'Jesus shall
reign where'er the sun'.

Watts was born, the eldest of nine children, in Southampton where
his father, a clothier of modest means, was a deacon at the Independent Chapel and, at the time of Isaac's birth, in gaol for his beliefs.
Isaac had a first-class education at a grammar school run by the rector
of All Saints church and a doctor offered to finance his time at either
Oxford or Cambridge. This he declined, since it would have meant his
becoming an Anglican.

Aged just 16, he complained to his father that the psalmody at the
chapel, where Calvinism dominated, contained nothing of the Chris-

tian gospel and little to excite wonder and adoration. His father responded by challenging him to do better and this set him towards Christian hymnody.

On completion of his education at a Dissenting academy in Stoke Newington in North London, where he sang in the choir, he returned home and spent the next two and a half years writing hymns. In 1699 he took up the assistant pastorship of Mark Lane Chapel in London, succeeding to the pastorate three years later. This was an influential post – a brother in law and a granddaughter of Oliver Cromwell were in the congregation – and he remained there for the rest of his life, though for most of this time he had frequent periods of absence owing to ill health.

His first book of hymns was *Horae Lyricae* (1706) and this was followed a year later by *Hymns and Spiritual Songs*. An enlarged edition of this contained 345 hymns and 15 doxologies, and in 1715 a small volume *Divine Songs for Children* was published. Finally, in 1719 a curious, less than satisfactory, Christianized version of the Psalter appeared.

It was not to be expected however that such a massive output of hymnody would be of equal quality. Erik Routley, a great admirer, said that his hymns 'scaled the greatest heights and plumbed the most bathetic depths'. Calvinism appears in an extreme form and the hymns are not always cheerful:

> Hark! from the tombs a doleful sound,
>   my ears attend the cry,
> 'Ye living men, come view the ground
>   where you must shortly lie.
>
> 'Princes, this clay must be your bed,
>   in spite of all your towers;
> the tall, the wise, the reverend head
>   must lie as low as ours.'
>
> Great God, is this our certain doom?
>   And are we still secure?
> Still walking downward to our tomb,
>   And yet prepare no more?

Grant us the powers of quickening grace
  to fit our souls to fly,
then, when we drop this dying flesh,
  we'll rise above the sky.

This was originally set to the tune of *Home, sweet Home.* Yet 'Give us the wings of faith to rise', 'Lord of the worlds above' and 'There is a land of pure delight', in company with many others, are timeless. Soon after his death a memorial bust was placed in Westminster Abbey, a statue was erected in London and a memorial hall built in Southampton.

Philip Doddridge (1702–51)

Philip Doddridge, a friend of Isaac Watts, was the twentieth child of his family and, following the death of his parents, was brought up by a Dissenting pastor in St Albans. In 1723 Doddridge became the pastor of an academy in Leicester and later transferred to a chapel in Northampton from where he exercised an influential ministry throughout the Midlands. He wrote several books rejecting the dogmatism of Calvin, and one of these was responsible for the conversion of William Wilberforce to evangelical faith. He also wrote many hymns, of which 370 were published after his death. All were intended to be sung after a sermon and were prefixed by a biblical text. 'Hark the glad sound! the Saviour comes', for Advent, and 'O God of Bethel, by whose hand' remain popular.

John Newton (1725–1807)

John Newton first won attention as a slave trader who had a conversion experience after reading St Thomas à Kempis's *Imitation of Christ* and surviving a storm at sea. He nonetheless continued his slave trading until, under the influence of George Whitefield, an early Methodist evangelist, he studied for the Dissenting ministry. In the event he was ordained into the Church of England's ministry and became vicar of Olney, in Buckinghamshire, in 1764. While there he began to compile a hymn book, not for use in church but in evangelical cottage meetings, held later in the great room of the manor house. *Olney Hymns*, as it came to be known, was initially a joint enterprise with his lay assistant, William Cowper, who contributed the first 67 hymns. Newton completed the task with a further 280 and the book, one of the earliest hymnals, circulated more widely.

Of the six Newton hymns included in *Common Praise*, 'Glorious things of thee are spoken' and 'How sweet the name of Jesus sounds' are deservedly popular, but best known of all is 'Amazing Grace how sweet the sound' which was virtually unknown by Anglicans until it became 'Top of the Pops' for nine consecutive weeks in the 1970s. It then had to be included in all new hymnals.

William Cowper (1731–1800)

William Cowper, John Newton's colleague, was the son of a rector of Berkhamstead. Having studied law, he was called to the Bar, and became commissioner of bankrupts. Soon afterwards however he suffered an acute bipolar breakdown from which he never fully recovered. Thereafter his life was punctuated by long periods of depression, and it was while he was in a private asylum, run by an evangelical, that he had a conversion experience. One consequence of this was that he became intensely devout and expressed his religious feelings in hymns of great poetic beauty. Of these, five are included in *Common Praise* – 'God moves in a mysterious way' (words which have entered the common English vocabulary), 'Jesus, where'er thy people meet', 'Hark, my soul, it is the Lord', 'O for a closer walk with God' and 'Sometimes a light surprises'. He also became one of the most important poets of his time and Samuel Taylor Coleridge regarded him as the best.

Charles Wesley (1707–88)

Charles Wesley had a creative partnership with his older brother, John (1703–91) in the foundation of Methodism. John engaged in an extraordinary preaching ministry that took him to every part of the British Isles, travelling over 200,000 miles on horseback and preaching an estimated 40,000 sermons. Enthusiastic congregations were formed wherever he went – mainly but not exclusively in the new industrial areas and the remoter rural areas where the Church of England had been specially negligent. Although an Anglican priest, he was not permitted to preach in parish churches, so his ministry was exercised out of doors or in halls and houses.

The preface to the 1933 *Methodist Hymn Book* began 'Methodism was born in song', indicating that, apart from preaching, the chief ingredient of its worship was hearty and fervent hymn singing, expressing corporately the vibrant faith of the believers. In the provision of this vital element Charles Wesley was without peer and became the greatest of all English hymn writers. While his brother was always on the move, he remained largely in London and Bristol, no less compulsively writing hymns and poems. The exact number of these is unknown and it is not always possible to draw a distinction between the two, but an astonishing 8,989 have survived – an average of three every day for 57 years. Some of these, together with the work of others, appeared in a series of hymn books spread over 47 years.

The latest edition of *Hymns Ancient & Modern, Common Praise*, has 39 hymns by Wesley – the largest single-author contribution to the book. A high proportion of these are very well known and loved and it is necessary to mention only 'Hark! the herald angels sing', 'Love divine, all loves excelling', 'Forth in thy name, O Lord, I go', and 'Ye holy angels bright' to indicate their universal appeal. But none was sung in the Church of England until many years after his death.

John and Charles, children of the very large family of a Lincolnshire rector, were public school educated and both went to Oxford where they started what became the Methodist movement. They were ordained into the Church of England's priesthood and both declared that they would never leave its ranks, though John eventually took steps (of which Charles disapproved) that would inevitably lead to schism. Samuel Sebastian Wesley, the foremost church musician of the nineteenth century, was a grandson of Charles and, besides great anthems, composed some fine hymn tunes, the most notable being *Hereford*, which is inseparable from his grandfather's 'O thou who camest from above' and *Aurelia* for S. J. Stone's 'The church's one foundation'.

CHAPTER FIVE

The Victorian Writers and Composers

Many hundreds of Victorians tried their hands at hymn writing and one musicologist has estimated that during the 60 years of Queen Victoria's reign as many as 400,000 hymns were written. After long years of verbose and often dreary experiences of worship, the Church of England awakened to the possibility of offering to God praise, thanksgiving and the deepest faith experiences in accessible words and singable tunes. This liturgical revolution was initiated not by careful scholars, but by pastors to meet a spiritual need.

Hymn writing became almost a craze among the more literary-minded clergy, though many laypeople, including Prime Ministers and their Cabinet colleagues, as well as some serious poets, also tried their hand. Inevitably the vast output was of varied quality and most of it – mercifully as it now seems – disappeared leaving little trace. But some was good enough to provide indispensable, much loved, items in every hymn book and to have a considerable influence on Christian worship and devotion. Among the most significant were:

Reginald Heber (1783–1826)

Reginald Heber was a Hanoverian rather than a Victorian, but demands inclusion as he is often described as 'the father of the modern hymn book', and also wrote some superb hymns. The son of Yorkshire landed gentry, he had a brilliant academic career at Oxford and won several poetry prizes. He was ordained in 1804 and immediately became rector of Hodnet, a family living in Shropshire where he remained for the next 18 years. Soon after arriving in the parish he decided that hymns could be useful for illustrating the Bible readings in the Sunday services and drawing the congregation more closely into the worship.

Being a High Churchman, he did not regard the evangelical hymns then starting to be circulated as suitable for this purpose, and in any case he needed something for every Sunday of the liturgical year. So he made a collection of 98 hymns, 57 of which he wrote himself, and his friend H. H. Milman, a future dean of St Paul's provided 'Ride on, ride on in majesty' for Palm Sunday. The remainder included the work of some of the greatest English poets, but neither the Bishop of London nor the Archbishop of Canterbury was prepared to authorize the book's use.

Heber's own hymns included 'Holy, holy, holy! Lord God Almighty!', 'Bread of heaven, on thee we feed' and 'Brightest and best of the sons of the morning', though this was excluded for a long time from some hymn books on the grounds that it encouraged the worship of a star. Excluded from virtually all modern hymn books is his once popular 'From Greenland's icy mountains', the second verse of which hardly encourages inter-faith dialogue, while it might be thought that the heathen are now somewhat nearer to us than Ceylon's isle:

What though the spicy breezes
    Blow soft o'er Ceylon's isle,
Thou every prospect pleases
    And only man is vile:
In vain with lavish kindness
    The gifts of God are strown,
The heathen in his blindness
    Bows down to wood and stone.

It is to be remembered however that beliefs of this sort inspired men and women to heroic missionary endeavour during the Victorian era.

Heber's hymn writing came to an end in 1822 when, against his personal inclinations, he was persuaded to become Bishop of Calcutta, For the next four years he was an exemplary missionary bishop, travelling widely, preaching, confirming and encouraging the small expatriate Christian congregations. It was after one of these exhausting journeys that he sought to cool down in a swimming pool and died from drowning, having had a stroke. In the following year his widow manage to persuade the Archbishop of Canterbury to authorize the use of the hymn collection.

Henry Francis Lyte (1793–1847)

Henry Francis Lyte, immortalized as the author of 'Abide with me; fast falls the eventide', also wrote the hardly less admired 'Praise, my soul, the King of heaven', based on Psalm 103, and 'God of mercy, God of grace', based on Psalm 67. He was only a 27-year-old curate when he heard a dying friend pray 'Lord, abide with me' – words reflecting Luke 24.29, where during the evening of the Resurrection day some of the disciples, walking to Emmaus, invited the incognito Jesus to spent the night in their home, with the words 'Abide with us, for . . . the day is far spent'. This led him to compose some verses on this theme which he kept to himself until shortly before his own death, when he gave them to a relative who had them published afterwards. The original version had three additional verses, 3–5, which were subsequently omitted from most hymn books.

Lyte, the son of a naval captain, was born in Scotland but soon the family moved to Ireland where at Trinity College, Dublin he won poetry prizes in three successive years. A curacy near Wexford led to a breakdown in health and, although he recuperated in the more hospitable climate of Cornwall, he was dogged by ill health for the remainder of his life. He was nonetheless able to spend 25 years as vicar of a new parish in Lower Brixham in Devon, and frequent trips abroad for health reasons were financed by his wife, the heiress of a rich Irish clergyman. He died from tuberculosis in Nice just a few months after his resignation from the parish. The popularity of 'Abide with me' undoubtedly owes much to the inspired tune *Eventide* provided by W. H. Monk.

John Henry Newman (1801–90)

There is hardly a better way of influencing posterity than that of writing specially fine hymns set to singable tunes. John Henry Newman, a major nineteenth-century theologian and the pioneering leader of the Church of England's Oxford Movement, is most famous for his conversion to Roman Catholicism – a move that shook Victorian England and was acknowledged by appointment as a cardinal. He was beatified by Pope Benedict when he visited Britain in September 2010.

But although Newman made no attempt to write hymns and did not wish his poetry to be sung, he is responsible for three of the most notable hymns still in use. These continue to influence for good the worship and devotion of churches of every tradition worldwide.

'Firmly I believe and truly' and 'Praise to the Holiest in the height' were extracted by enterprising hymn book editors from Newman's long, dramatic poem *The Dream of Gerontius* in which an old monk, who has led too worldly a life, approaches death and is now repentant. The content of the poem often suggests a depressive authorship and much of the underlying theology is questionably Christian. But in 1900 the composer Edward Elgar, turned it into a deeply spiritual oratorio which is now regarded as one of the masterworks of the twentieth century. Elgar's music was not however used for the hymn tunes.

'Lead, kindly light, amid the encircling gloom' is different. Newman, having been struck by a serious illness while visiting Italy in 1833, had a frustrating journey back to England. A three-week wait for a boat at Palermo in Sicily, was followed by further delay when the Marseilles-bound vessel was becalmed for a week in the straits separating Corsica from Sardinia.

It was during this time that he wrote a poem which expressed his physical exhaustion – 'The night is dark, and I am far from home; lead thou me on.' – and possibly the beginning of the agonizing spiritual struggle that would eventually take him into the Roman obedience. As a hymn, it became immediately popular after its publication in the appendix to the first edition of *Hymns Ancient & Modern*, and it was read to Queen Victoria as she lay dying.

Newman, the son of a rich London banker, was born in 1801. After a brilliant academic career at Trinity College, Oxford he became a fellow of Oriel College, was ordained in the Church of England and subsequently appointed vicar of St Mary's – the university church in Oxford – where his intellectual gifts and deep spirituality made him the leading light in the Oxford Movement. His influence on the revival of the Catholic element in the Church of England's life cannot be exaggerated.

Following his reception and ordination into the Roman Catholic Church in 1845 he remained in Rome for 18 months before returning to England to establish in Birmingham a branch of the Oratorian Order, of which he remained a member until his death in 1890. From 1854 to 1858 he was rector of Dublin University.

Cecil Frances (Fanny) Alexander (1818–95)

Cecil Frances Alexander is often described as 'the Queen of children's hymn writers', though her three best-known and most used hymns – 'All things bright and beautiful', 'Once in royal David's City' and 'There is a green hill far away' – are loved by every age group. They were designed to explain the articles of the Apostles' Creed and first appeared in 1848 in her collection *Hymns for Little Children* which had a preface by John Keble. The profits from its 100 impressions went to support a school for deaf and dumb children.

The third verse of 'All things bright and beautiful' has now been omitted from *Common Praise* and many other modern hymn books lest it be thought to encourage social and economic inequality:

The rich man in his castle,
  the poor man at his gate,
God made them, high or lowly,
  and ordered their estate.

London schools were forbidden to use it in the 1960s.

Like many hymn-writers of her time, Fanny Alexander's output was prolific. Her *Hymns for Little Children* also included a hymn which begins 'Do no sinful action, speak no angry word', which remained in common use until comparatively recently. Like many other Victorians, her thoughts often turned to the subject of death. Thus her children's hymn which opens 'Within the churchyard, side by side, are many long low graves' ends with resurrection hope:

So when the friends we love the best
  lie in their churchyard bed,
we must not cry too bitterly
  over the happy dead;

Because, for our dear Saviour's sake,
  our sins are all forgiven;
and Christians only fall asleep
  to wake again in heaven.

Although only one of her compositions was included in the first edition of *Hymns Ancient & Modern*, there were 18 in the 1889 supplement, seven of which had been specially commissioned. Few of these have survived, but *Common Praise* naturally includes her top three, together with a magnificent versification of *St Patrick's Breastplate*, 'I bind unto myself today'. There is also 'Jesus calls us: o'er the tumult' for St Andrew's Day.

Mrs Alexander was born in Dublin into a military family and her father, on his retirement from the army, became a land owner and agent. She was a member of the Church of Ireland and influenced initially by the Oxford Movement and later by the evangelical views of her rector. In 1850 she married a young clergyman, William Alexander, who served in a number of parishes of increasing importance; in all of these she worked assiduously among the sick and the poor during a time of great economic and social hardship in Ireland.

In 1867 her husband became Bishop of Derry and Raphoe and they spent the next 28 years in what he described as 'an opulent prelacy with extensive patronage' in the city of Londonderry. The duties of a bishop's wife, however, precluded more hymn writing and when Dr Pusey suggested a second collection of children's hymns she declined. The disestablishment of the Church of Ireland in 1869 did however provoke her to write an uncharacteristically angry hymn which begins:

Look down, O Lord of heaven, on our desolation!
  Fallen, fallen, fallen is now our Country's crown,
dimly dawns the New Year on a churchless nation,
  Ammon and Amalek tread our borders down.

At her funeral in 1895 crowds lined the streets of Londonderry; four months later her husband was elected Archbishop of Armagh. By this time he was displaying some signs of hymn-weariness and told a church congress in Swansea, 'I speak only for a minority of the clergy – those who have never made, and who never intend to make, a collection of hymns.'

John Mason Neale (1818–66)

John Mason Neale owes his considerable reputation to a remarkable gift as a hymn translator. From the outset the proprietors of *Hymns Ancient & Modern* planned to include hymns from the pre-Reformation centuries and, since these were invariably in Latin or Greek, the services of translator with a poetic sensitivity were essential. With Neale they could not have done better and one eighth of the contents of the first edition were his work – either translations or his own compositions. Thirty of these remain in the much larger *Common Praise*, including, in translation, 'O come, O come, Emmanuel', 'All glory, laud, and honour', and 'O what their joy and their glory must be'. Many were the work of the earliest hymn writers and a good example of his genius is the compline hymn that dates before the eleventh century:

Before the ending of the day,
Creator of the world, we pray,
that with thy wonted favour thou
wouldst be our guard and keeper now.

From all ill dreams defend our eyes,
from nightly fears and fantasies;
tread under foot our ghostly foe,
that no pollution we may know.

O Father, that what we ask be done,
through Jesus Christ thine only Son,
who, with the Holy Ghost and thee,
doth live and reign eternally. Amen.

Neale, the son of an evangelical clergyman and brilliant mathematician, was himself the best classical scholar of his year at Trinity College, Cambridge and won many poetry prizes. At Cambridge he came under

High Church influences and, following his ordination in 1841, ran into difficulty with bishops because of his views. In 1846, however, he managed to be appointed warden of Sackville College, East Grinstead, in Sussex – a charity home for 30 people which was outside the jurisdiction of the Bishop of Chichester. There he rebuilt the dilapidated chapel, furnishing it on High Church principles, formed the Society of St Margaret – a religious order for women dedicated, initially, to nursing – and extended the charity's work to include an orphanage, a girls' boarding school, and a home for 'the reformation of fallen women'. Some of this work continues today in London, Sri Lanka and the USA.

Neale spoke 20 languages and from 1851 to 1853, by which time he had a wife and five children to support, augmented his meagre income by writing three leading articles a week for the *Morning Chronicle*. In addition to his hymnody he wrote many books on church history, liturgy, patristics, the Eastern Church, and for children. He died when only 48.

Catherine Winkworth (1827–78)

Catherine Winkworth was different again and, more than anyone else, was responsible for the introduction of German hymnody into England. To her we owe the translations of 'Now thank we all our God', 'Praise to the Lord, the Almighty, the King of creation', 'Jesu, priceless treasure', 'Christ the Lord is risen again' and five other items in *Common Praise* – almost all with German tunes. She was a daughter of a London silk merchant who moved to Manchester. There she spent most of her life, came under Unitarian influence, and devoted a good deal of her time to work among the poor of the slums. The Prussian ambassador to London, Karl Josias Bunsen, to whom she was introduced, gave her a copy of a German devotional book which included hymns, and he encouraged her to study German in Dresden.

She now began to collect German hymns which she translated, with considerable poetic skill, into English. Under the general title *Lyra Germanica*, 103 of these were published in 1855 as *Hymns for the Sundays and Chief Festivals of the Christian Year*, and another 121 in 1858 as *The Christian Life*. The first volume ran to 23 editions and the second to 12. These were followed by *The Chorale Book for England* (1863) and *The Christian Singers of Germany* (1869) – a study of German hymn writing from the ninth century. She was also active in the movement for women's rights and, as secretary of the Clifton Association for Higher Education for Women, played an important part in the foundation of what became Bristol University.

Joseph Bacchus Dykes (1823–76)

Joseph Bacchus Dykes was precentor of Durham Cathedral from 1849 to 1862, then vicar of St Oswald in the same city until driven to resignation by a serious physical and psychological breakdown in 1876. This was undoubtedly caused by the unwillingness of the evangelical Bishop of Durham to licence curates to the large parish because of its vicar's High Church beliefs.

Most of Dykes's 300 hymn tunes were composed before he became overwhelmed by pastoral responsibilities. Seven of these were accepted for the first edition of *Hymns Ancient & Modern*, another 24 were taken into the 1868 supplement, and 56 more into the 1878 edition. Many had been commissioned to suit particular hymns and when these were of inferior quality – over-sentimental, narrowly subjective or depressingly gloomy – the music proved to be much the same.

One of Dykes's specialities was a hymn with a short final line which he emphasized by dragging out, sometimes excruciatingly. Thus Ralph Vaughan Williams was ruthless in his choices for the *English Hymnal* in 1906 and accepted only six Dykes tunes for the main book and five more, reluctantly because of their popularity, for the 'chamber of horrors' appendix.

The proprietors of *Hymns Ancient & Modern* dispensed with some in their later editions, but 22 survived into *Common Praise* and there can be no disputing the quality of those attached to 'Holy, holy, holy! Lord God Almighty!', 'Eternal Father, strong to save' and 'Praise to the Holiest in the height'. Of the others, those for 'The King of love my shepherd is', 'We pray thee, heavenly Father' and 'Jesu, the very thought of thee' are probably the most used. Even though he had a great love of music, and Durham University made him an honorary D.Mus., he always said that his work as a priest was more important to him. Following his death in 1876 the Bishop of Durham raised £10,000 for the support of his widow and children.

Arthur Sullivan (1842–1900)

Arthur Sullivan was a very different character, famed for his comic operas and colourful love life. But he also composed some good hymn tunes of which the curiously named *St Gertrude* for 'Onward, Christian soldiers' is easily the best known. There are also tunes for the Easter 'Alleluia! Alleluia! Hearts to heaven and voices raise', the harvest 'To thee, O Lord, our hearts we raise', and an adaptation of an English traditional melody for the Christmas 'It came upon the midnight clear'. Sullivan was in fact one of the best known Victorian composers and composed 13 major orchestral works. It irked him that his popularity rested on his collaboration with the librettist W. S. Gilbert on *The Pirates of Penzance*, *The Mikado*, *HMS Pinafore* and other Savoy operas.

He was a son of a military bandmaster, became a chorister at the Chapel Royal and had an anthem published by Novello when he was only 13. He then studied at the Royal Academy of Music and in Leipzig before becoming organist and choirmaster of then fashionable St Michael, Chester Square in London's Belgravia. The tenors and basses in his choir were however all policemen. He was in constant demand for choral and orchestral works and his Victorian spirit was expressed unforgettably in the music of *The Lost Chord*. Queen Victoria knighted him in 1883 and on his death ordered that he should be buried in St Paul's Cathedral.

Ralph Vaughan Williams (1872–1958)

The Victoria age had only just ended when there emerged a composer who would become one of England's three greatest of the twentieth century, the others being Edward Elgar and Benjamin Britten. And it was the great good fortune of English hymnody that in 1904 Percy Dearmer was inspired to invite him to become the musical editor of the new *English Hymnal*. He had not yet become famous and was specially interested in English folk songs, making a collection of these that eventually topped 800. Having studied under Charles Villiers Stanford and Charles Wood at the Royal College of Music, he started to earn a modest income as organist of St Barnabas, South Lambeth. He had only recently moved from atheism to what he called 'cheerful agnosticism', where he remained for the rest of his life.

Experience as a church organist turned him against Victorian hymns – 'More often than not they are positively harmful to those who sing and hear them.' So, faced with the *English Hymnal* challenge, he chose about 50 English traditional melodies and carols: 'Fight the good fight' was given an adapted version of a folk song *Tarry Trousers*, while 'Who would true valour see' was allocated a folk song he had picked up in the Sussex village of Monks Gate. Not all his choices quite suited the words and some were thought to be frivolous, but the linking of the church's folk songs with their secular counterparts added something new and refreshing to hymnody. Many are among the 37 items under his name in *Common Praise*, but none can match the sheer beauty of his own *Down Ampney* (the place of his birth in Gloucestershire) which he composed for 'Come down, O Love divine'.

CHAPTER SIX

Pop Goes the Hymn Tune

Although the title *Hymns Ancient & Modern* was perfect for the nineteenth century, it was less appropriate for the book's 1950 edition inasmuch as the overwhelming majority of the hymns once described as modern belonged to the Victorian era. The first half of the twentieth century was not a period of prolific or innovative hymn writing, though some valuable items appeared.

In 1955 however things began to change and before long there was another, still flowing, torrent of hymn writing and composing comparable with that of the previous century. In October of that year a broadcast from Martock parish church, in Somerset included a new hymn tune, *Chesterton*, of an idiom quite different from that of the past. Its composer, Geoffrey Beaumont, was a priest of the Community of the Resurrection, working in a tough Southwark parish in Camberwell. He had a flair for composing light music and the tune reflected this. In the following year his setting of the Eucharist in the same idiom, broadcast from St Augustine, Highgate attracted considerable interest. With it were a few hymn tunes, including a 'swinging' version of 'Now thank we all our God', and many enterprising parishes adopted the new style, including drums, guitars and saxophones.

Next, Patrick Appleford, the Youth and Education Secretary of the United Society for the Propagation of the Gospel, composed a *Mass of Five Melodies*, together with several new hymns, and became a leading light in the formation of the 20th Century Church Light Music Group. This informal group of authors and composers, lay and ordained, had the declared aim of 'producing and promoting the use of new hymns and new music in the worship and teaching of the church'. They saw this primarily as a means of furthering the church's mission, and defended the ephemeral, arguing that hymns had a contemporary usefulness and need not therefore be aimed at posterity. Among the most outstanding of the many who followed were:

Sydney Carter (1915–2004)

Sydney Carter emerged at about the same time and quickly became known throughout the English-speaking world for his *Lord of the Dance*, adapted from an air of the American Shaker movement. More a song than a hymn, this has not discouraged its use for occasions as diverse as weddings, baptisms and funerals, as well as many other acts of worship when something lively and singable is needed. It is now a 'must' for any hymn book. Also included in *Common Praise* is his 'One more step along the world I go' – another jaunty item, expressing a joyful optimism.

Carter was himself a gentle, humble man, a pacifist who had served in the Friends' Ambulance Unit during the war. But he was not an amateur musician and by the time *Lord of the Dance* brought him world fame he was already established as a leading writer and singer of folk songs. Many of these were about social issues, particularly the quest for social justice, and his liberal outlook expressed to perfection the spirit of the 1960s.

Fred Kaan (1929–2009)

Fred Kaan, a prolific hymn writer, was also in this territory. Indeed, so securely that a famous MP, Enoch Powell, was driven to speak in the House of Commons of his concern about a version of the Magnificat:

Sing we a song of high revolt;
make great the Lord, his name exalt!
Sing we the song that Mary sang
of God at war with human wrong.

Sing we of him who deeply cares
and still with us our burden bears.
He who with strength the proud disowns,
brings down the mighty from their thrones.

By him the poor are lifted up;
he satisfies with bread and cup
the hungry ones of many lands;
the rich must go with empty hands.

He calls us to revolt and fight
with him for what is just and right,
to sing and live Magnificat
in crowded street and council flat.

Mr Powell would doubtless be relieved to know that the hymn did not win a place in *Common Praise*, but this may have been for poetical rather than political reasons.

Kaan was born and brought up in Holland where his father was involved in wartime resistance to the Nazi occupiers. In 1955 however he moved to Britain to be ordained into the Congregational ministry, and it was while serving at the Pilgrim Church in Plymouth that he became frustrated by the official church hymn book's lack of what he regarded as suitable material for the Sunday services. So he compiled a supplement of his own hymns and continued to write when he became an executive secretary of the World Alliance of Reformed Churches in Geneva, and subsequently Moderator of the West Midlands Province of the United Reformed Church. One hundred of his hymns were published in *The Only Earth We Know* but, although he is recognized as an important ground breaker, only two of these were taken into *Common Praise*. There is a fine Eucharistic hymn, 'Now let us from this table rise' and the deservedly popular 'For the healing of the nations', with its call to God for the banishing of 'pride of status, race or schooling' and of 'dogmas that obscure your plan'.

Timothy Dudley-smith (b. 1926)

Timothy Dudley-Smith provided a more elegant, gentler and now widely used version of the Magnificat – 'Tell out, my soul, the greatness of the Lord' – which, while remaining faithful to the original, nonetheless declares, 'Proud hearts and stubborn wills are put to flight, the hungry fed, the humble lifted high'. This is one of his 19 works in *Common Praise* – making him the fourth largest contributor after Charles Wesley, Isaac Watts and John Mason Neale.

He belongs firmly to the evangelical tradition and, prior to his retirement, had editorial and leadership roles in the Evangelical Alliance and the Church Pastoral Aid Society before becoming Archdeacon of Norwich, then Suffragan Bishop of Thetford. He had long written poetry but it was only when his friends began to put his poems to music that his hymn-writing potential emerged. Much of his earlier work was written during family holidays in Cornwall.

Eschewing the choruses of the evangelical charismatic movement, his style is uncompromisingly traditional, yet his hymns express the Christian faith in new and often refreshing ways. Over 300 of them are in about 250 hymnals worldwide and, usefully, they provide something for every season of the liturgical year. No less usefully, they have been allocated attractive, singable tunes.

Erik Routley (1917–82)

Erik Routley made only a small direct contribution to Anglican hymnody (six items of words and music are in *Common Praise*), though his harmonization of an Irish traditional melody *Slane* for 'Be thou my vision, O Lord of my heart', and 'Lord of all hopefulness, Lord of all joy' places him among the most widely used. His contribution to the study of church music, and hymnody in particular, was however without peer in the twentieth century.

He combined the gifts of a scholar with the art of a musician, and the power of a brilliant communicator. A lecture, illustrated by himself at the piano, was an experience to be savoured. He wrote no fewer than 21 books on church music, was music editor of *Congregational Praise* (1951), and wrote another 14 books on a variety of biblical and theological subjects.

Hymns and Human Life (1952) was, and remains, a book of great importance, displaying exact scholarship in its history of hymnody and strong personal opinion in its judgements. Near the end of his life *A Panorama of Christian Hymnody* (1979) was a massive addition to the understanding of the subject, and in the same year he published *An English-Speaking Hymnal Guide*.

Routley enjoyed an international reputation. After spells of teaching church history at Mansfield College, Oxford and ministry at important Congregational churches in Edinburgh and Newcastle upon Tyne, serving also as president of the Congregational Union of England and Wales, he became, in 1975, professor of church music at the Westminster Choir College, Princeton in the USA.

He said that a good hymn must pass two tests: 'as a piece of craftsmanship in literature it must be without blemish' and 'if it is not the kind of thing a congregation can sing, being more suitable for personal devotion, and if it is not praise that is addressed to God and dealing with the things of God, it fails'. Wider adoption of these criteria would reduce considerably the amount of published hymnody.

Hence the challenge facing the editors of all hymn books at a time when the flow of new hymns was unceasing. The 1950 edition of *Hymns Ancient & Modern* was essentially a refining of the choice of pre-1939 hymnody, and too early to take account of even the beginning of the forthcoming renaissance. By the end of the 1960s, however, the proprietors were driven to publish *100 Hymns for Today* (1969) which contained mainly new hymns – those of Sydney Carter, Patrick Appleford, Fred Kaan and other contemporary writers – but also 'The Lord's my Shepherd' to the tune *Crimond*, Percy Dearmer's 'Jesus, good above all other', and a few other old favourites, some of which had been released from copyright.

Such was the liberal, social action content of many of the new items that Archbishop Michael Ramsey suggested mischievously that the book would be useful for students of the Church's ancient heresies. This did nothing to limit its popularity and a second volume, *More Hymns for Today*, was published in 1980. Both were incorporated as a supplement into *Hymns Ancient & Modern New Standard* (1983).

Meanwhile. the editors of all the other established hymn books were making their choices from the new material for new editions and a considerable number of new books began to appear. Special provision was needed for some of the revivalist-type hymns, choruses and songs that flooded out of the evangelical charismatic movement; song sheets and overhead projectors were employed to encourage spontaneity and whole-hearted singing in the churches that used them.

As the century's end approached, the Council of *Hymns Ancient & Modern* recognized the need for a revision of their book that required more than an updating of what had gone before. A Hymn Book Committee, under the chairmanship of Professor Sir Henry Chadwick, a distinguished Patristic scholar and also a musician, was entrusted with this task and produced an entirely new book which still contained hymns both ancient and modern. Just over 50 by contemporary writers and about the same number by contemporary composers were included, and there was a new title, *Common Praise*. This associated it with *Common Worship* (2000), the Church of England's new liturgical book which it was designed to complement.

Given the degree of liturgical diversity now evident in the Church of England, it was however apparent that no single hymn book could meet the needs of every congregation. Size alone made this impossible, and there was the further point that, although much new material was widely used and deservedly popular, some had an ephemeral character that made it unsuitable for inclusion in a book designed to last quite a long time. In 2010 therefore *Hymns Ancient & Modern* and the Royal School of Church Music expressed a new and thriving partnership in the publication of *Sing Praise*. Consisting of 330 hymns, songs and other short musical items, all of fairly recent vintage, this provides a considerable variety of items for churches where predominantly new hymns are used, though it will be welcomed also by other parishes requiring more than *Common Praise* was able to find room for. It is in fact designed to complement *Common Praise* and space has been made available for more women writers and more young writers.

CHAPTER SEVEN

Faith, Hope and the Future

Bishop Stephen Platten

A member of the Council of Hymns Ancient & Modern Ltd

1851 saw the opening of the Crystal Palace in Hyde Park, Joseph Paxton's 'eighth wonder of the world' at the heart of the Great Exhibition. With the enthusiasm and imagination of Prince Albert propelling it, the Great Exhibition heralded a new world: it also put Great Britain and the Empire as the brave pioneers. Out of this same world, less than ten years on and following that conversation on a GWR railway carriage, bubbled *Hymns Ancient & Modern*. That name conceals how revolutionary the initiative was. Trevor Beeson has shown this in his earlier chapters. Nothing like it had existed before and it assisted the liturgical revolution which had issued from the Tractarian movement. The hymn book was, we have seen, a Tractarian, a 'High Church' enterprise. Now, rather like the Governors of *Hymns Ancient & Modern*, remarkably the Commissioners of the Great Exhibition still exist and still meet. Their task is very different but it remains one of encouraging innovation, heralding new worlds. *Hymns Ancient & Modern* has similarly transformed itself more than once. Such change is vital.

The 'Church's folk songs' have themselves recently undergone rapid change. Up until the 1980s hymn books looked much the same as ever, but the world was moving on. The charismatic movement gave birth to a completely different genre of worship songs. Simple choruses, often repeated and increasingly backed by drums, electric guitars and other instruments were one sign of this. Then there was also the liturgical movement. Already, in the Church of England, the Eucharist was rapidly unseating sung mattins as the main morning worship. In the 1960s a new Liturgical Commission started its work; no longer was it the *Book of Common Prayer* or nothing at all.

The market dominance of *Hymns Ancient & Modern Revised* and the *English Hymnal* began to be challenged. In 1982 Hodder and Stoughton (as it still was) published *Hymns for Today's Church*. Not long after this arrived the much greater challenge of *Mission Praise*. It is easy to demean it, but goodness it was popular! Beginning as a flimsy paperback in response to Billy Graham's 'Mission England', it expanded and improved itself. Now it is a 1000 plus collection of hymns used by many churches across the traditions, including many Anglican congregations. Hotfoot, in 1986, came Kevin Mayhew's *Hymns Old and New*; it did not adopt that name by accident! It was a direct challenge. Again it has become popular and often in Anglican churches too; in 2000 it became *Complete Anglicans Hymns Old and New*. Mayhew is a Roman Catholic, Billy Graham a Baptist. Hymnody is now truly ecumenical.

But the revolution was not over. Two further innovations helped speed change. First was the increasing popularity of screens in worship. Instead of congregations having their eyes firmly locked on to a hymn book page, now entire churches look skywards, watching words and music dance across a white screen. The second radical shift which also engaged with the proliferation of screens was the revolution through I.T. and the Internet. Increasingly liturgy became instant. Like fast food it was easily obtained, put together with a simple menu and cast into the bin at the end of the service. Both these developments (the computer could also compose liturgy for the screens) meant that in many instances hymn books became obsolete.

Trevor has shown how *Hymns Ancient & Modern* (HA&M) responded to its rivals: *Hymns Ancient & Modern New Standard Edition* and *Common Praise* were new initiatives. They remained, however, firmly in the traditional mould. Even *Lambeth Praise*, published by HA&M for the 2008 Lambeth Conference feels like and looks like the hymn books we have all come to know and love. HA&M has concentrated on what it knows it can do well. Even *Sing Praise* stands in that tradition. The quality of lyrics and music remains high; the production standards are outstanding. This still means hymn books which are a joy to use. Indeed so much is this so that other churches – the Church of Scotland, the Irish Presbyterian Church and the Methodist Church in England have chosen HA&M as their publishers. Nevertheless more change was presaged and the company happily had its prophets!

In many ways the most radical shift came in 1975. It was the brain-child of the financial proprietor Edgar Bishop and his colleague in management, Gordon Knights. What had happened previously? Well, up until July 1975, HA&M had been run as a loose-knit proprietorship. It was entirely independent of the church establishment and contained as its proprietors names with which to conjure, both in the Church of England and in the world of sacred music. So, the centenary history of *Hymns Ancient & Modern* contained in an appendix a list of the proprietors. Sir Henry Baker, the founding musical father heads the list. Bishop Frere, co-founder of the Community of the Resurrection, former Bishop of Truro and prominent liturgist is there. Sir Sydney Nicholson, founder of the Royal School of Church Music comes later in the list as does Canon Lowther Clarke, Edward Gordon Selwyn, sometime Dean of Winchester and John Dykes Bower sometime organist of St Paul's Cathedral. Still, however, A&M remained a loose association. It was the genius of Edgar Bishop and Gordon Knights to transform this association into a company by incorporation, *Hymns Ancient & Modern Ltd*.

As we shall see, this did not stem the flow of outstanding proprietors, but it did allow for astonishing new developments. The trick was, of course, to form a company which could be the kernel to develop a more diverse enterprise. *Hymns Ancient and Modern New Standard* was the first hymn book edition to be published by the new company. More intriguing still, however, was the emergence of Canterbury Press Norwich, an entirely new publishing imprint under whose auspices was published the *New English Hymnal* in 1986. Canterbury Press opened the door to much broader publishing opportunities and indeed, under the editorship of Christine Smith, it has become one of the most successful publishers of liturgy, spirituality and popular religious titles in Britain; the increase of turnover has been remarkable. Canterbury Press has taken full advantage of the diverse possibilities afforded by the Church of England's Liturgical Commission's *Common Worship* project: this would eventually herald new possibilities of cooperation as we shall soon see.

But alongside home-grown imprints, the capital accrued over the past century or more presented the new company with opportunities for acquiring new titles. So the *Religious and Moral Education Press* was bought from the de-merging Pergamon group; for close on twenty years RMEP provided a publishing service for schools both for religious education syllabuses and also collective worship; only recently, with significant changes in buying for education, was the imprint discontinued. Perhaps the boldest move was the acquisition of the *Church Times* in 1989. This weekly newspaper, founded in 1863, was the leading journal for news, comment and reviews for the Church of England. It had been in the hands of the Palmer family throughout its existence for 126 years, and now the proprietor Bernard Palmer sought a buyer who would be sympathetic to its aims and audience. Over the past 18 years Paul Handley has worked with the tradition but also broadened the scope of the newspaper, transforming it for a changed culture. As well as the *Church Times*, other periodicals have been added to the list: *The Sign*, an inset for parish magazines remains a popular perennial; *Third Way* came under the umbrella just three years ago now and is a thoughtful, attractive and provocative monthly aimed at a younger audience.

Perhaps the next key milestone was adding SCM Press to the family in 1997. SCM Press was born of the Student Christian Movement, a liberal and ecumenical organization established in the early part of the twentieth century and owing much to the vision of one Tissington Tatlow. The movement prospered most in the years after the Second World War. SCM people had offered energetic and thoughtful chairmanship of the board of the Press: these included Trevor Beeson, David Jenkins and later still Derek Haywood. The Press also had a series of inspired editors including David Edwards (later Dean of Norwich and Provost of Southwark) and John Bowden. Bowden's remarkable skill set included business acumen, theological scholarship, linguistic skills (he translated from a number of languages) and publishing flair. It was he who negotiated its independence from the SCM, and he too who sent out envoys to HA&M. He realized that the company was undercapitalized and saw HA&M as the most obvious partner and parent. With SCM Press, the incipient group gained the most prestigious theological publisher in Britain. It had been responsible for an unparalleled list in biblical theology. It had brought Moltmann, Pannenberg and later Hans Küng to the theological market in the English-speaking world. It also showed a sense of courage in publishing controversial titles. Both John Robinson's *Honest to God* and later *The Myth of God Incarnate* were SCM titles: Don Cupitt remains an SCM author.

More recently there has emerged a partnership with the Royal School of Church Music which is mutually nourishing: the RSCM now cooperates on new hymn book projects. Most recent of all has been the bringing of Church House Publishing under the wing of HA&M: production, marketing and much of the editing is now fully integrated into the book publishing arm of what is a burgeoning, if modest, group of companies. This expansion has also led to another growth point in the broadening of our wholesaling and warehousing/distribution arm in Norwich Books and Music; in 2010 a new, significantly larger warehouse facility was leased further from the centre of Norwich. This has enabled a very considerable development of the distribution business which broadens the base of the group's activities and increases the contribution made to the wider church. Even as this book was being produced, agreement was reached with the Church of Scotland so that St Andrew Press, with its impressive backlist and continuing new publications, has now added to the publishing arm of the group. All of these developments have been nourished by the development of websales and an integrated website which also includes the other acquisition not yet mentioned, Church House Bookshop. This retail shop means that the group now has a high street (well almost high street!) presence at the heart of the Church of England's administration and next to the seat of its synodical government.

This expansion and development would have been unimaginable without the entrepreneurial and commercial expertise of three outstanding chief executives. We have already seen the remarkable and innovative contribution of Gordon Knights. Gordon's foresight transformed a hymn book publishing board into a thriving group of book, hymn book and periodical publishing imprints. With Gordon's retirement in 2004, we were fortunate to recruit Andrew Moore as Chief Executive. Andrew brought with him a wealth of experience. Having had a senior management role at Marks and Spencer and having also worked with Delia Smith, he contributed much to the integration of the different divisions in the group. His energetic work as a Methodist layman meant that he was able to spot other gaps in the breadth of our market base. This brought *Third Way* into the list of periodicals published by the group. Andrew retired in 2008, and Dominic Vaughan came as our new Chief Executive. Again he brought significant experience in commerce and publishing. Following his work with the Elsevier Group and then the Royal Pharmaceutical Society, Dominic has developed the integration, expansion and business base of HA&M further still.

None of this would have been possible without recruiting a remarkable and loyal staff, some of whom we have mentioned. None of it would have been possible without a continuing tradition of distinguished proprietors, now normally known as 'governors' or directors. Paramount among them was the outstanding scholar, Professor Sir Henry Chadwick, who chaired the board during the earlier part of the expansion which we have described. At that time he worked with a number of accomplished church musicians – Chadwick himself started out as a musician. Among his colleagues were the late Dr Lionel Dakers, sometime Director of the RSCM and Dr Allan Wicks, sometime organist of Canterbury Cathedral. Working with these too was Sir Richard O'Brien, a businessman who had been director of the government's Manpower Services Commission and who later chaired the commission which produced the controversial and prophetic report *Faith in the City*, a report which was formative in two successive governments' approach to urban renewal. Before his retirement Professor Chadwick recruited Patrick Coldstream, who eventually succeeded him as chairman of the board. Patrick brought with him the skills of a *Financial Times* journalist and businessman; he had also chaired an ecumenical commission which produced an influential report by the churches on unemployment. He was ideally suited to take on the responsibility for the further growth and expansion of the group. The diversification of the company's activities mean that it is no longer necessary to include a director with specific musical background; our links with RSCM give us an excellent entrée into that world. On a different front, we have benefited greatly from Alan Morton's contribution as a director. Alan was for many years the company's accountant and joined us on his retirement from full time accountancy work.

Any history of *Hymns Ancient & Modern* would be incomplete without mention of its charity status and its charitable giving. The aims of the company are the furtherance of the Christian religion. These aims are achieved both through publishing and through charitable giving. Profits are ploughed back into the company and also disbursed as grants in two distinctive ways. First, grants are made to churches wishing to re-equip their hymn book stocks or wishing to change to one of the hymn books published by HA&M. But secondly there is a wider remit to the company's charitable giving. The annual figure for giving is modest on the scale of some charitable foundations and it varies to some degree as the vagaries of the market and trading conditions affect the profits.

But where has the focus been with giving? Predictably there has been a focus on church music and on education: choirs, colleges with a church music bias and other musical agencies have benefited from grants. Some specific projects of an ecological or social nature have been supported, as have on occasion publications which have been deemed important but which required a subvention to make them viable. Two other principles have been applied. First, since the sums available for disbursement are relatively small, we have sought to support projects where a modest sum will make a real difference. Secondly, we have regularly supported some institutions whose aims are very specific and will not satisfy secular grant-making foundations. Two examples are the Irish School of Ecumenics and the Anglican Centre in Rome.

Trevor Beeson began this brief history with a conversation between two collectors of hymns on a journey on the Great Western Railway in 1858. From that conversation came the germ of the idea which led to the publication of *Hymns Ancient & Modern* in 1861. That was in itself a seed for revolution. The past thirty years have seen a further revolution (or even a series of revolutions) equal to that first initiative. Innovation will not stop here, as the Commissioners of the Great Exhibition, ten years before *Ancient & Modern* was first published, saw so clearly. They continue, as do we. What innovations will A&M be celebrating on its bicentenary? How too can we continue to contribute to the growth of good hymnody, while promoting a better understanding of the Christian faith?